Caimans

By Sam Dollar

Steadwell Books

Raintree Steck-Vaughn Publishers

A Harcourt Company

Austin · New York
www.steck-vaughn.com

ANIMALS OF THE RAIN FOREST

Published by Raintree Steck-Vaughn Publishers, an imprint of Steck-Vaughn Company.

Library of Congress Cataloging-in-Publication Data
Dollar, Sam.
    Caimans/by Sam Dollar.
        p.cm. -- (Animals of the rain forest)
        ISBN 0-7398-3097-X
        1. Caimans--Juvenile literature. [1. Caimans. 2. Endangered species] I. Title.
II. Series

QL666.C925 D66 2000
597.984--de21   00-33813

Printed in the United States of America
10 9 8 7 6 5 4 3 2 1 W 02 01 00

Produced by Compass Books

Photo Acknowledgments
Crocodile Specialist Group/Godshalk, 22
Kevin Schafer, cover
Root Resources/Mary and Lloyd McCarthy, 4–5, 16
Visuals Unlimited/Joe McDonald, title page, 26;
   Cheryl A. Ertelt, 8, 24; Rob & Ann Simpson, 11;
   Fritz Pölking, 12, 19, 20; N. Pecnik, 29

Content Consultant
Dr. James Perran Ross
Crocodile Specialist Group

Contents

MEXICO
BELIZE
HONDURAS
GUATEMALA
EL SALVADOR
NICARAGUA
COSTA RICA
PANAMA

Caribbean Sea

VENEZUELA
GUYANA
SURINAME
FRENCH GUIANA (FRANCE)

North Atlantic Ocean

COLOMBIA

ECUADOR

AMAZON RIVER

PERU

BRAZIL

BOLIVIA

South Pacific Ocean

CHILE
PARAGUAY

URUGUAY

ARGENTINA

South Atlantic Ocean

Range of the Caimans

6

A Quick Look at Caimans

What do caimans look like?

Caimans are crocodile-like reptiles with long snouts and tails. They can be green, gray, brown, or black.

Where do caimans live?

Caimans live in South America and Central America. They live near water in rain forests.

What do caimans eat?

Caimans eat only meat. They eat any animals they can catch.

Do caimans have any enemies?

Anacondas and jaguars are the only animals strong enough to kill adult caimans.

Caimans use their sharp teeth to kill and eat other animals.

Caimans in the Rain Forest

Caimans are large reptiles that live only in the rain forests of South and Central America. Caimans, alligators, crocodiles, and gavials make up the crocodilian family. Scientists grouped these animals into one family because they have features in common. Caimans are a great deal like alligators that live in the United States.

Caimans and other crocodilians have long snouts. They have strong jaws and sharp teeth. Their eyes and noses stick up a little above their heads. This helps them see and breathe while they are swimming. Crocodilians have long, strong tails. They have skin between their toes. These webbed feet help them swim fast.

Where Caimans Live

There are six kinds of caimans. Many caimans live in Amazonia in South America. Amazonia is the largest rain forest in the world.

Caimans are amphibious. This means that they live in water and on land. Caimans live in wet habitats. A habitat is a place where an animal or plant usually lives and grows. Caimans can live in freshwater rivers, lakes, small streams, and flooded forests. They also live in swamps and marshes.

Caimans are cold-blooded. Cold-blooded animals have blood that is about the same temperature as the air or water around them. Temperature is how hot or cold something is. Caimans bask to raise their body heat. Bask means to lie in the sun.

During hot, dry weather, caimans need to lower their body heat. They swim to cool themselves. They also dig tunnels or large holes in the ground. These tunnels and holes are called burrows. The cool mud of the burrows lowers their body heat.

▲ **Caimans keep only their noses and eyes above water as they float.**

Many caimans are nocturnal. Nocturnal animals move around most at night. Caimans stay in their burrows during the daytime. They come out at night to hunt.

Caimans' coloring helps them blend in with their surroundings. This camouflage makes caimans hard to see.

Special Body Parts

All caimans have thick, strong skin. The skin's color depends on the type of caiman. Caimans can be green, gray, brown, or black.

Like all reptiles, caimans have hard scales. These hard pieces of skin cover and protect their bodies. Scales hold in caimans' body heat. They keep caimans from drying out while they bask. Round plates of bone called osteoderms are beneath the scales. These small bones on caimans' backs and stomachs are like armor.

Caimans have special body parts that help them swim. An extra eyelid that is clear covers their eyes. This lets caimans see the animals they hunt for food underwater. Flaps of skin seal their nostrils, ears, and throats when they dive underwater. The flaps allow them to hunt and eat underwater without drowning.

Caimans use their teeth, jaws, and tails to fight other animals. The teeth on their lower jaws curve inward. These specially shaped teeth help caimans hold on to animals that are trying to escape. The muscles that snap caimans' lower jaws shut are very strong. They can easily smash through hard turtle shells.

Kinds of Caimans

The six kinds of caimans all have things in common. But each one is slightly different.

Black caiman is the largest kind of caiman. A male can be 15 feet (4.5 m) long. It has dark skin with gray stripes on its lower jaw. Yellow or white bands cover its body. The bands fade as the caiman grows older. The black caiman has larger eyes and a thinner snout than other caimans.

Broad-snouted caimans are medium sized. The largest ones grow to 11.5 feet (3.5 m). They have light olive-green skin. Sometimes they have spots on their lower jaws. This kind of caiman has a wider snout than any other kind of caiman. They hunt mainly snails and turtles in the water.

The common caiman received its name because it lives in more places than other caimans. It is also known as the spectacled caiman. It has a bony ridge between its eyes that looks like a pair of spectacles or glasses. These caimans can grow up to 8 feet (2.5 m) long.

The Cuvier's dwarf caiman is the smallest kind of caiman. A male grows only about 5 feet (1.5 m) long. Cuvier's dwarf caimans have brown skin and brown eyes. They have black bands on their bodies and white bands on their lower jaws. Their snouts are short and turn upward. They spend much time cooling off in water.

The Jacare caiman can grow up to 10 feet (3 m) long. It is also known as the piranha caiman. Piranhas are South American fish with sharp teeth. The Jacare caiman has large teeth in its lower jaws. These teeth stick up farther than other caimans' teeth do.

The Schneider's dwarf caiman can grow up to 7.5 feet (2.3 m) long. It is sometimes called a smooth-fronted caiman because it has no bony ridge on its snout. It spends its days in water or in burrows. It hunts along rivers at night.

Caimans eat fish, birds, other reptiles, and large animals such as deer.

Hunting

Caimans are carnivores. A carnivore eats only other animals. Caimans will eat almost anything they can find. They even eat dead animals or other caimans if they cannot find food. Animals that caimans hunt and eat are called prey.

A caiman's food changes with its habitat. For example, broad-snouted caimans stay in water more than other caimans. They eat mostly snails, fish, turtles, and other animals that live in water.

A caiman's food changes with its age. Young caimans eat insects, fish, and turtles. Adult caimans eat larger, hard-to-catch prey such as wild pigs.

Territories

Each adult caiman has its own territory. This space along the water's edge is close to the caimans' burrows. At night, caimans hunt in their territories.

A territory may be large or small. The size depends on how many caimans live in the place. Caimans sometimes share their territories with other caimans.

Hunting and Eating

Caimans hunt mainly by sitting still and waiting for prey to come near. When caimans swim, they keep only their eyes, ears, and noses above water. They can hear, smell, and see prey this way. But it is hard for animals that live on land to see them.

Caimans quickly charge at prey when prey is close enough. They bite and hold it with their teeth. Then they shake prey back and forth until the prey dies.

Sometimes caimans hunt together. They form a line across small, slow-moving streams. They

These caimans are working together to catch fish.

block the stream and lie in the water with their mouths open. Caimans catch fish in their mouths as fish try to swim past them.

Caimans use their teeth to tear chunks from their prey. They swallow these chunks whole. Caimans swallow stones and other hard things. These things stay in a caiman's stomach to help break down food.

▼ Young caimans are born during the rainy season when the forest floods.

A Caiman's Life Cycle

It takes caimans 7 to 20 years to grow large enough to mate. After this, caimans mate every year or two for about 20 years. Over the course of her life, a female caiman may have hundreds of young.

Caimans mate during the beginning of the rainy season. During this time, rain falls every day. The floor of the rain forest floods. During mating season, males make special roaring sounds to attract females. Male and female caimans may chase each other. Sometimes males fight each other to mate with females.

Young caimans hatch during the rainy season. To live, caiman young need to catch food in the flooded forest. Water and food are too hard to find during the dry season.

This female caiman is staying close to her nest to protect it.

Nesting

After mating, the female builds a nest for her eggs. The place a caiman picks depends on the type of caiman. Some caimans hide their nests. Some build their nests in the open, and some build nests on river islands.

The female builds a nest with fresh plants, leaves, grass, and mud. She uses her back feet and tail to move this material into a large pile. Then she walks over the pile to press it down.

The female lays eggs in an open space at the top of the nest. Females lay from 10 to 60 eggs. The number of eggs depends on what kind of caiman it is. Females cover the eggs with grass and mud. This hides the eggs and keeps them warm. Young caimans grow inside the eggs for about three months.

Females stay close to their nests to keep their eggs safe. Predators such as foxes, lizards, and monkeys will attack caiman nests for food. Common caiman females will sometimes share a nest. This makes it easier to fight predators.

> This young Jacare caiman must take care of itself. It is basking on a log.

Hatchlings

A young caiman rubs its snout against the shell when it is ready to hatch. A sharp bump on its snout makes a small hole in the shell. This bump is called a caruncle or egg tooth. The caiman pushes its snout through the small hole.

It fights its way free of the eggshell. The new caiman is then called a hatchling.

Hatchlings make grunting noises. The noises tell the female that her young have hatched. The female returns to the nest to dig away the mud and grass. She helps the hatchlings out of the nest. Then she leads them to water.

Each kind of caiman raises its young differently. Some caimans do not raise their young. Other caimans keep the pod in the female's burrow. A pod is a group of hatchlings. Until they grow older, the pod travels together and hunts together.

Predators eat many young caimans. Caimans are most likely to die during the first few months or years of life. Only a few caimans live to be adults.

Adult caimans live from 20 to 30 years or more. Few predators are strong enough to kill an adult caiman. Only jaguars or anacondas can kill adult caimans.

Caimans have a large range in the rain forest because they can adapt and will eat almost anything.

Living with Caimans

Caimans are good at adaptation. Adaptation is a change a living thing goes through to fit in better with its environment. Caimans can live in many different habitats. They will eat any animals they can catch.

Caimans can live in different temperatures. They have ways to raise and lower their body heat. This allows them to live in many places with different kinds of weather.

Today, there are many caimans in the rain forest. Caiman numbers are healthy because people are working to keep caimans safe.

Hunting Caimans

Some people hunt caimans for their skins. They use the skins to make things like boots and belts. Caiman skin is not as valuable as alligator or crocodile skin. One caiman skin is worth about $20. One alligator skin is worth about $150.

Today, special farms raise caimans for their skins. Caiman farmers sell about 500,000 caiman skins each year.

Governments control the number of caimans that people can hunt. Venezuela, Guyana, and Nicaragua let people hunt caimans. Some native people eat caimans as food.

Destruction of the Rain Forest

Caimans depend on their rain forest habitat to live. They eat, mate, and live there. Caimans might die out if their habitat is destroyed. If caimans die out, other plants and animals could be hurt, too.

For example, common caimans are helpful to the rain forest. The waste that comes out of their bodies helps plants grow. This allows fish to eat and survive.

Some people hunt caimans.

Some companies are mining metals and minerals from the rain forest. Waste from the mining sometimes flows into rivers. This can kill caimans.

All living things are an important part of life in the rain forest. Rain forest destruction puts caimans in danger. Caimans could be lost forever if the rain forest continues to be destroyed.

Glossary

Amazonia (am-uh-ZONE-ee-uh)—the largest rain forest in the world

amphibious (am-FIB-ee-uhs)—able to live on land and in water

burrow (BUR-oh)—a tunnel or hole in the ground dug by an animal

carnivore (KARN-uh-vor)—an animal that eats only other animals

habitat (HAB-i-tat)—the place where an animal or plant naturally lives and grows

hatchling (HATCH-ling)—a young animal that has broken out of its shell

osteoderms (OST-ee-oh-derms)—the plates of bone underneath a reptile's scales

pod (PAHD)—a group of animals that lives and hunts together, such as caimans

predator (PRED-uh-tur)—an animal that lives by hunting other animals for food

prey (PRAY)—animals that are hunted and eaten by other animals as food

Internet Sites and Addresses

Crocodilians—Natural History and Conservation
http://www.crocodilian.com

The Discovery Channel
http://www.discovery.com

The Gator Hole
http://www.home.cfl.rr.com/gatorhole

Crocodile Specialist Group
Florida Museum of Natural History
University of Florida
Gainesville, FL 32611-7800

Rain Forest Action Network
221 Pine Street Suite 500
San Francisco, CA 94104

Index